Girl, Get Yo' Life!

A Young Woman's Guide for Life & Relationships That Win

RACHELLE L. LAWSON, M.A.

Girl, Get Yo' Life!

A Young Woman's Guide to Life and Relationships That Win

Rachelle L. Lawson, M.A.

All Rights Reserved

Copyright © 2019 Rachelle L. Lawson

No part of this book may be reproduced or transmitted in any form or by any means, electronic or mechanical, including photocopying, recording, or by any information storage and retrieval system without express written permission of the author.

Cover image licensed by Shutterstock

ISBN: 9780578452326
ISBN-13: 978-0-578-45232-6

Printed in the United States of America

First Edition

For information about special discounts for bulk purchases, speaking engagements or workshops for your organization,
please contact:
At The Table Communication, LLC
atthetablecommunication@gmail.com
614-600-2143
www.rachellelawson.com

DEDICATION

To the little sisters that I never had, the daughters I never birthed, my goddaughters, my nieces, great nieces and granddaughters to come. To my communication students across Ohio... Be empowered to live more fully and freely. You CAN!

TABLE OF CONTENTS

	Acknowledgments	i
1	Introduction	1
2	The Masterful Plan	9
3	Authentically You	15
4	Qualify Your Circle	23
5	Your True Self, Representative or Imposter	29
6	You Are Not An Accident	35
7	Your Perception is Your Reality	43
8	Speak Love to Me	47
9	Sticks, Stones and Words that Hurt	55
10	To Complete or Compliment	63
11	Everyone Wins	69
12	Conclusion	75

ACKNOWLEDGMENTS

If I had 10,000 tongues, I could not thank you enough. Thank You, Father God, for loving, calling, choosing, forgiving, and sending me forth with a message from your heart. Your grace IS sufficient for me. I love you!

My Family:

Many thanks to ALL of my family for sharing your lives and experiences and support throughout my lifetime. I am eternally grateful for all of you.

Mama and Daddy: The best of everything you had, you gave to me. For that I am eternally grateful. Mama, it's a privilege to have YOU as both my natural and spiritual Mother. God Bless You RICHLY!

Jarius and Jeremiah: I love you and live for you. You keep me going and always call me to a higher standard. My life would not be the same without you. Stay true to yourself, authentically. Don't be moved by culture or peers. Your grace is in your gift.

Stephen Lawson: Thank you being the influence that you have in my life. You shared your knowledge of Upward Bound with Mama and Daddy and my life shifted drastically. I am grateful for you. I love you.

Stephania Lawson Banks: Thank you for always being my consummate encourager. You listen and share your wisdom and energy without hesitation. You have taught to be firm in what I believe and not to compromise. Thank you for being my friend, listening ear, sister in the natural and in the faith. I love you to life!

Lisa Lawson: Thank you for your honesty, wisdom and for always holding me to a higher standard. You always point me back to the Father for everything and there's no better place. God Bless you. I love you to life!

Bryan Lawson: My big brother. Thank you for being my counselor and friend. You are the realest, most honest, straight shooting, compassionate, brilliant man I have known. You taught me how to work hard and make it look like play. You taught me about relationship compartments, me how to run those numbers and how to be present! Make it count! I Love You forever! R.I.P. "What up, Haaauuusss!" "Everything's good!" "Good. Better, Best. Never let it rest 'til the good gets better and the better gets best!" "Alriiiighty!"

Alya Lawson: Thank you for being my hype man, for listening to me go on and on about my passion. I appreciate you for being yourself, confidently, sharing your ideas, wisdom and pushing this project. Girl, Get Yo'Liiiife!!

My Spiritual Mentors:

My life would not have been the same without your influence, honesty, integrity and truth lived out before me. Thank you all for allowing God to use you as examples of a real women of faith, strength, courage, grace, love and power.

Denise Harris

Brenda Oliver

Michelle Christian

Cynthia Armstrong

Dr. Cheri Westmoreland

Minister Vanessa Slater: Thank you for being my mentor, sister, my confidant and friend. For living the truth of God's Word aloud before me. You always challenged me see myself differently and to embrace the new truths that I discovered. Thank you for teaching me to serve and sow into the lives of other. You empowered me to do, be and live an enriched life in Christ. I am eternally grateful for you in my life and Jarius'. Thank you for timeless lessons that I hold dear and countless prayers over my life. I love you!

Diane Brown: Thank you for being the truest example of a woman who lives freely, with reckless abandon in Christ. You are gift to the body, and I am grateful to have you as a mentor and sister. You taught me about discipline and ALWAYS asked me the tough questions without judgment, but with grace. Thank you!

Marcia Futel: Thank you for your friendship, leadership, wisdom, honesty, mentorship and support. You always pulled me higher and caused me to see myself differently. Thank you for supporting me in His Truth when I was unsure and for cultivating the seeds/gift in me.

Elder Jerry Culbreth: My teacher, friend and pastor. Thank you for pouring from your immense overflow into my life week after week, session after session. Your passion for God's Word is infectious and my life has been ever enriched by your presence in it. You are a tremendous gift to the body of Christ. There is none like you. Thank you!

Dr. Eleanor Bolar: Where do I begin? Thank you for being my mentor, sister, teacher and friend. You have been an example of honesty, faithfulness, integrity, and grace. I am so grateful for you allowing me to blossom in your presence. Thank you for being an ear of wise counsel day after day for decades. I admire your strength and fearlessness. Your voice was instrumental in the manifestation of this project. When I thought I could not write 100 pages you said "You just talked 100 pages in the last 2 hours of conversation!" Here it is! I love you to life!

Minister Donnise Wise: Thank you for seeing me before I saw myself, for teaching me how to live God's word and to properly position myself to pray and receive. I appreciate your commitment to me and Hannah's Daughters. I love you!

Janell Jones: My sister and Biz Bestie, you have inspired me from the airport until this day. Thank you for pushing me and holding me accountable to my dream.

Mia Redrick: Thank you Coach Mia for your direct, truthful approach to coaching. I appreciate you for helping me to see myself as I am and for holding space for my bigness. As you breathed, God used your breath to clear out the cob webs that clouded my view. Thank you for helping me see my possibilities!

University of Cincinnati Upward Bound Program: Thank you Mr. Myron Hughes, Dr. Cynthia King Partridge and Mr. Philip Cathey for your love and support. You give so much of yourselves to the cause of children and education. Thank you for putting up with me, years ago. It took me a while, but I'm turning the corner.

UC UB Alpha Psi Omega: Y'all know we were a brilliant, one of a kind group of teens and worked well together as a team (for the most part). Thank you teaching me how to love, give my all, be supportive and step with the best of them. We went through so much together, but I believe that our lives are better today because we had each other then. I am forever grateful for all the you are and have been in my life. YOU ARE IRREPLACEABLE. I love you to life! Thank you all!

Nicole Williams
Deania Carson
Lisa Meatchem
Furaha Cathey
Tamiko Engleman
Tonjarene Bronston
Victoria Franklin

Ricarla Boyden
Tyree Gaines
Carmelita Casey
Michelle Franklin
Helaine Wilson
Angelea Underwood

Jerome Kimber: My dear friend without whom, my life would not be the same. I am eternally grateful for your sharing God's Word and love, for seeing me in my future and affirming my beauty and Queendom. Thank you for every effort you made to live God's word aloud. It did not go unnoticed. I miss you greatly and love you always. R.I.P.

Shardae Postway: Thank you for always sharing your life, letting me into your heart, hearing my heart, sharing God's word and the message this work and my life. You are a treasure, gifted, brilliant and wise.

Angela Wallace: Thank you for being my promoter, visionary and hype woman. You see my heart and believe in me in a way that is indescribable. Thank you for sharing your life, heart, experiences, and faith with me. You are a tremendous woman; brilliant, beautiful and loved. Your gifts make room for you, Girl! I love you, Sis!

1 INTRODUCTION

Though we may not have the same life experiences, human nature allows us to understand and relate to one another, in some ways. The circumstances may differ, but the impact can be the same.

 -Rachelle Lawson

My Story

Like any other family type, growing up in a large family has its advantages and disadvantages. My family was a traditional rule-based family where children did as they were instructed with minimal questioning if any at all. The interesting dynamic is that I am the youngest of my parents' eight children. Because of the age span between me and my siblings, I was like an only child for many years. While they were all moving out, getting married, raising families, attending colleges, graduating from high school and building businesses, I was still in elementary school. This challenged me. I was so much younger than everyone else that I didn't have the opportunities to really connect and grow with them, nor from them, until much later in life.

Social networks are an important part of one's development and life. This is especially true for those in single parent or only child households without close sibling relationships. One component that was missing from my life very early on was self-awareness. Although I learned a level of who I was and what I could add to others, what I did not understand was how my difference was valuable. Both at home and school, I was rarely affirmed. I was good at some things, but not much or where it seemed to matter. I had a nice singing voice, played instruments, was good at Double Dutch and I could teach others how to do what I knew. My younger friends often looked up to me. I tried sports like the other kids, but I wasn't fast on the track, couldn't get that tetherball in my favor, struck out in softball, etc.

Beyond that, I often wondered what life was all about. At a young age, I wondered about these things. What was the meaning of it all? In my world, life seemed to be somewhat futile, at a deep level. Sure, I enjoyed playing with my friends, but I spent quite a bit of time alone. I didn't know where my place was. I was trying to FIT IN when, in fact, I was BORN to stand out! But how?

In high school, my brother introduced me and my parents to the Upward Bound (UB) program at the local university. It is a college preparatory program for first-generation college students, offering year-round tutoring, academic classes, stipends, activities, college tours, and pre-collegiate courses. Here is where the trajectory of my life shifted and began to take shape.

The program was like a home away from home for many students. We were like-minded kids who were equally ambitious, yet in need of support and guidance academically. What we also found were friendships that were cultivated in a safe environment with a leadership team that was experienced, tough and compassionate.

Like many adolescents, the sounding board for most ALL my life decisions became my "all wise and all knowing" friends. Granted, we were a pretty smart, intelligent and wise group of kids. However, we were just that… Kids. Teenagers, no less. We brought all our experiences, knowledge, abilities, personalities, beliefs and values to the table and formed a sisterhood organization within the UB program. We were just about EVERYTHING to one another. We lived together, ate together, worshipped together, traveled together, fought together, studied together, created together, achieved together, partied together and loved together. We were fortunate to have what many do not, sisterhood. It sustained me through high school and into college.

It was my desire to attend a Historically Black College or University (HBCU), however, my family did not have the resources for me to go away to college. Instead, I attended my local university as a commuter student. My major was education, as I knew that I wanted to teach because that was something that I was good at as a child. There was still a lack of assurance and direction in my life. My friends would tell me things that I was good at and how I supported their lives, but I had no idea what to do with that information. What I had was a deep longing for more of life! More meaning. More substance. More fulfillment. More influence. More impact. I simply wanted to be more, give more and receive more from life.

When I became a Christian and developed a relationship with God, I began to know myself more intimately and began to satisfy the questions I longed to have answered. I understood more of the meaning of life, my purpose and the role I play in the cycle of life. What enlightenment! How empowering is it to know that *you* were designed and *sent* to fulfill a specific plan in life? Very much so! *My* identity as an individual connects back to where I came from, originally: the mind of the all wise, all knowing, ever present, creative God!

I am reminded of the movie Lion King. After Mufasa, King of the Pride, was trampled and killed by the stampede of wildebeests, his son Simba was to succeed him. Simba was deceived to believe that he caused his father's death and left the pride. While in exile, he grew and tried to deny his identity; it was inside him, however, and he could not escape it, though he tried. Upon learning the truth of his identity and position in life, he returned to the pride to walk in his purpose as King Simba.

It was the same for me. Understanding who I am as an individual, my design, my nature, and my value-add, directly impacts my purpose in the world. Likewise, who I am, and my purpose directly impacts the relationships I have with others. Nothing is by chance. I became a lifelong student of myself. I took courses to help me uncover my identity. Once I became a little clearer on who I was, I studied more to discover my purpose. At each level, I had more confidence and peace within.

After taking these courses and learning about Rachelle, I decided to take a break from school to work full time. My responsibilities changed since I had become a new mother. I received an associate degree in Education. With the new addition to my life, I still needed to be sure about where to go next on my journey because it would directly affect my child. After a few years, I became disillusioned with my job and began preparing for my next move. The icing on the cake happened when I enrolled in a course at the university called Interpersonal Communication. OMG! It was everything I loved and knew!

You see, my family and I love to learn and teach. We could ALWAYS be found gathered around the dining room table in deep conversations. We discussed everything from philosophy and psychology to spirituality and nutrition/health, from relationships to business. We often discussed how we could better serve our circle of influence and be the change we want to see. All the conversations we had at the table about people and how we relate to and interact with one another, prepared me for the study of it in school. The communication course was incredibly engaging. Every area of it, from chapter to chapter, page to page, had my full attention.

The following fall quarter, I resigned from my position and enrolled as a full-time student of communication at the university. During my senior year in college, I thought I would enjoy a role as a high school counselor, so I applied to graduate programs in psychology. After interviewing several faculty members within the discipline, I found that it was NOT what I expected and therefore NOT for me. One of my favorite professors in my program department strongly encouraged me to pursue a master's degree there. That is exactly what I did and although I did not fully understand God's plan, I have not regretted it once. All things were working together for my benefit. Girl, I was getting my life!

These years of self-discovery and living in new truths proved to be some of the best years of my life. Walking more freely in myself, without compromise or envy is empowering. Knowing my mission and purpose in life, how I add value to others and make a difference is empowering. Understanding that every relationship is not meant to be for a lifetime, but some are only for a moment in time is equally empowering. They are meant to help us grow into higher versions of ourselves and to add more value to our relationships with others. This kind of relational exchange is powerful and enriching, to say the least. My life is not perfect by any stretch of the imagination, nor is it void of pain, strife, challenges, or misfires. But I am better equipped with the tools—in my resource belt of life—than ever before. When I veer off the path in the wrong direction, I am more quickly able to make my way back to the main road. Why? Because I have seen and understand more about myself, where I belong and what is not good or right for me.

In every relationship I have, from the waiter at my favorite restaurant to students in the courses I teach, from my children to the young woman at the bus stop, from my friends to business associates, I endeavor to give the best of myself and sow seeds of purpose in them. Because it was freely given to me, I can freely give it away.

What I Learned

Being a deep thinking, introspective person, I began my quest to learn more. The trajectory of my life shifted again when I came to know God and developed a relationship with Him. Now, I am not, by any means, saying that life has been perfect since then. It has not. But what it has been is meaningful!

1. My life is not by chance, but by design. Divine design, that is.

2. My identity, who I am, is not defined by my friends, culture, family or others. But by my Creator and me.

3. All my life experiences will be used together to impact or influence the lives of those in my circle or beyond.

4. Because we are created to be in relationship with one another and "do life" together, my life is not my own. My choices and purpose impact others directly or indirectly.

5. We are the common denominator in EVERY single relationship we have.

6. Many relationships are challenged because people are insecure in their identities and unfulfilled within themselves.

7. REALIZE who you are, EMBRACE/EMBODY your authenticity, ACCEPT your true self and LIVE more freely!

I Have Become Who I Once Needed

Of all my experiences, nothing gives me more pleasure than encouraging and empowering a young woman to be bold, courageous, self-aware, honest with herself, non-compromising, and influential. As an educator and communication scholar, I understand the value of imparting these ideas and values into women and girls. Not to take anything away from men and boys because they are equally valuable to the family and community.

The difference is in how we communicate, nurture and share within our families, friend groups and communities. In general, women talk A LOT. Although, not as much as men, we talk a lot, nonetheless. We share stories in detail, often finishing one another's sentences and thoughts. We advise more than asked, nurture one another, etc. Additionally, biologically, women have the life-giving womb within us. The womb is an incubator for life. Within this place, everything that is necessary for the implanted seed to grow and thrive exists. Once the seed is implanted into the soil of the womb, if you will, the seed begins to develop and multiply into a very masterful creation. Whatever seed a woman is given, will be received, nurtured and multiplied back to you. I believe that imparting seeds of knowledge, wisdom, grace, and hope into girls and women is one way to enrich lives and impact the entire world with the same. She will nurture it and ultimately multiply it into the image of the fullness of what the seed is designed to produce. It can create a positive ripple effect.

Be empowered in knowing that who you are innately, and your life assignment, DIRECTLY impacts your relationships. All your relationships. They affect your relationship with yourself, your friends, spouses, partners, children, employers, coaches, and even strangers. At the point of intersection where your lives connect, you bring all of you. Will you interact as your true self, your representative or an imposter? ***Girl, Get Yo' Life!***

GIRL, GET YO' LIFE!

2 THE MASTERFUL PLAN

You weren't an accident. You weren't mass produced. You aren't an assembly-line product. You were deliberately planned, specifically gifted, and lovingly positioned on the Earth by the Master Craftsman.

-Max Lucado

Have you ever asked yourself the questions 'Why on earth am I here?' or 'What is my purpose in life?' If you are a person who thinks about the greater meaning of life, then you've probably asked these types of questions. Guess what? You are not alone. Many people have spent their lives searching to 'find themselves' or discover their life's mission; ultimately searching for the purpose or meaning for their lives. We can ask ourselves the question 'why am I here?', but the more primary question is 'who am I?' The knowledge of who we are is critical to understanding our life's purpose. The late Dr. Myles Munroe said if we don't know the purpose of something, we will abuse it (abnormally use). This may be one reason that many people are unhappy and unfulfilled in their lives. They have yet to discover who they are and have done many things to "feel" their way through life without ever fully uncovering their purpose or true meaning for life.

Should we be concerned about who we are? Is it worth the time and effort to take the journey of self-discovery? Emphatically, Yes! Absolutely! Why, you ask? One reason is that every single interpersonal relationship that we have involves us. Every interaction we have with others is influenced by who we are. Each relationship is different. The people involved are different. The dynamics are different. The rewards are different, and the costs are different, as well as the needs of each person. Amongst those differences, one element is consistent: YOU! Every relationship begins with and involves you, the individual.

Wouldn't you agree that if every relationship, whether professional, personal, familial, and social, begins with us and includes us, then it is important for us to have a good sense of self or identity? Should we have some knowledge of who we are and be able to answer the question "Who am I?" How can we ever know the value we add to a relationship or partnership if we are unaware of ourselves? How can we know what we need from the relationship if we don't know who we are? Furthermore, how can we know what benefits we need or even what we want from a relationship without knowing what we are missing? We can't effectively answer these questions nor pursue fulfilling, healthy relationships without this knowledge.

Setting out on the journey of self-discovery is an amazing and liberating experience as you come to really understand who you are as an individual. We live in this culture and society that encourages us to be the same. Yet, we were created as *OUT*standing people. Our uniqueness makes us valuable. The difference we add to the world is the very thing that makes us valuable. Ofttimes, people will tease about or make jokes about people's differences, but that very thing that makes us different can be what has the greatest impact on those in your circle of influence and elsewhere.

In my estimation, many people are unhappy and unfulfilled within themselves, not only because they don't have knowledge of who they are or why they're created. It is that they have not embraced it. We cannot be something that we are not. We can only be the best version of ourselves. PERIOD! You cannot be anyone else. You can only be you because you don't have the same materials that others do, in the same quantities. As much as we try to suppress our natural inclinations to be what is acceptable, profitable, etc, the more our nature will rise.

Seeds possess the capacity to grow. That is what they do. Spring forth! If the seeds of your uniqueness are inside you, they will manifest. We don't understand that, which is part of the reason people try hard to fit in and to be accepted. Although there is value to having other people encourage, support, and validate you on some level, the reality is that we don't need that as we grow and develop an understanding of our identity. We have to realize who we are, embrace it and embody it.

God created us to be and live freely in that, but the challenge can be discovering the truth of who we are. We must peel back the layers of ideas and expectations of our family, friends, culture, and society. We must courageously throw off the expectations of those who think they will vicariously live their unlived lives and fix their failures through us. Loosen yourself from all those things that bind you so you can peel back the layers and live more freely!

One of my favorite movies is *Shrek*. In the movie, Shrek took Donkey to the auction block and Donkey escaped and tried to follow Shrek back to the forest. On the journey back to the forest, Shrek repeatedly told Donkey he could not go with him. Being obnoxious as he was, Donkey jumped around asking why he couldn't go. Sherk told him no again. They went back and forth a few times. Finally, Shrek replied to Donkey telling him that Donkey couldn't go because he was like an onion. An onion? Onion?! What he was implying was that he had layers to himself and he was not open to allowing Donkey to see them ALL. He could come so far before he got to know the fullness of who Shrek was… an Ogre! You see, when you peel back the layers of the onion, layer by layer, and get to the core, you are then able to really identify what that onion is made of. We, as individuals, are much like the onion. Layer by layer, level by level, we disclose our depth and breadth to others until they know us as intimately as we allow.

The process of self-discovery is not a race, but a marathon. You don't take one class and then confidently say you know all about yourself. It is a journey. However, getting on the path is both rewarding and empowering. To understand and learn about who you are is liberating. To be confident in walking in your authentic truth and intentionally pursuing purpose is empowering, to say the least. What do I do with all this newfound knowledge about who I am? What am I supposed to do with the gifts that God has given me? How can I serve others and live a fulfilled life? This is a large part of what life is all about.

We are created to serve God and to serve and fellowship with one another. This is one reason it is important to know who you are and what you bring to the table in your relationships. With this understanding, you can operate in your authentic self at a higher level of self-awareness.

One thing that I believe about people is that we can often identify fake behavior. We can tell when someone is disingenuous. It's part of human communication. We can recognize the nonverbal cues we see, so if you are not sure about who you are or why you are here, people can identify that. Be authentic. Life is a journey, so learn to embrace the truth of who you are and embody those characteristics as you master being the best version of yourself that you can be. The world needs all that you are and have to offer it. Suicide rates have increased, especially among young people. Hurting people hurt other people. A lack of hope and lost identity, not having accepted, nor embraced who they are individually and that they have influence and impact in the world and their relationships is painful.

God knows the truth about you, so Girl, get yo' life! and then give it away! Serve the world, your friends, your neighbors, your family, and your children. You can impact change and give hope to others. There is work to do in our families, communities, churches, schools and abroad.

Think about it, life can be quite overwhelming without others. We are not created to live alone and to carry the weight of the world by ourselves. We were created to support, love, and add value to one another as we fellowship in the earth. Knowing who we are, or at least having an idea, helps make life more fulfilling. It helps us to choose better for our lives. We cannot know who we are in totality because we are ever evolving, multilayered, multifaceted beings and life is a journey. However, knowing more about yourself in the true most authentic and pure place, the core of who you are, how God created you in your nature, in your mother's womb, is valuable and worth the time and process. He gave you life, gifts, passion, talents, preferences, abilities, and capacity for growth. He gave you vision. He gave you purpose. He built you. Like an architect and engineer work together to build a storefront strip mall or a skyscraper. The purpose is different, yet the builder has all the specifications and knows intimately what each building can withstand. He knows our frame, how we are made. He knows what we can handle, what we love and what we loathe. He knows if we are sensitive or not. He knows if we are tenacious or a quitter. He knows the depth of our makeup. As a result, He knows what we can carry, and He has expectations of us to use and pursue purpose based upon how He created us in his image and with His help. ***Girl, Get Yo' Life!***

3 AUTHENTICALLY YOU

"As you become clearer about who you really are, you'll be better able to decide what is best for you - the first time around."
-Oprah

For years, I have perceived that there is an identity crisis in our culture. People are hurting, lost, confused, insecure and disingenuous. Do you notice people as being fake, covering up their true identities to be accepted and liked? Our current selfie culture is consumed with perfection. People are looking for things to identify with. I believe this stems from not having clarity of who we are innately.

How can you know the true purpose of something without knowing the mind of the creator? The inventor, builder, developer, designer or creator has a particular purpose for the creation. They know of all the mistakes made in the production process. This is one reason that consumer products come with an instruction guide. For others to figure out what it is supposed to be or do, is not impossible, but can be challenging especially with no frame of reference. For example, a chair doesn't know that it is a chair, nor that it is to be sat upon. It doesn't know because it is the creation. Likewise, the universe is a creation. It does not know what it is designed to do or be aside from its creator. Any designer, developer, and creator knows the purpose for which they create, not the creation itself.

The same is true for us. We cannot fully know what we are made of, whether it's "sugar and spice and everything nice", "snips and snails and puppy-dogs' tails" or a combination, without searching inward to discover the clues left from the creator. Neither will we be fully able to understand our purpose in life without knowing the mind of our creator. There is evidence and there are clues inside of us, to who we are authentically. The seeds that God planted before creation are to be watered, nurtured, cultivated and expressed.

Whether we believe it, doesn't change that its truth. We are created by God. In the image and likeness of Christ, God created us before the foundation of the world. He knew us, created us and formed us with His creative fingerprint. He made each person both the same and different. Our fingerprints and DNA differ from billions of people on the face of this earth. How does that happen accidentally? It doesn't. We are created beings, purposed to be here on Earth in this dispensation of time, to fulfill an assignment in the cycle of life while serving one another in relationships and fellowship.

Identity Development

Identity is a fundamental part of life and relationships. Why do I suggest that? Every single relationship we have has one common denominator, its us. Each of us impacts every single relationship that we have including our relationship with bank tellers, waiters/waitresses, spouses, children, bosses, teachers, coaches or friends. Even, and most especially, the intrapersonal relationship we have with ourselves. What you say to yourself, believe about yourself and tell others about you, speaks more to your subconscious mind than anyone else. It is true that if you think you are, you are! If you think you can, you can! So, what are you thinking, Girl?

Being authentic is truly the ONLY way to live well, that is for those who desire to live full and free lives. It begins inside us individually. We must peel back the layers of familial, cultural and societal influences that have shaped our identity to discover and understand who we are and what we bring to relationships. How else can we have healthy relationships if we have not identified who we are and what we bring into the relationship with us? This foundational element of life and relationships is often left out of the equation.

There are different influences that impact how our identity is shaped. They are our creator from whom we originated, our authentic self (biology and seeds of individuality), our families and friends, our culture, our society, etc.

As you endeavor to get to know yourself, be encouraged to begin at the beginning with your creator. Getting to know God and how he fashioned you is empowering to every area of life. It supports you in making better choices in your career, relationships, business, education, etc.

When we meet someone new and desire to get to know them more, what do we generally do? You've guessed it! We invite them to coffee, an event or a phone conversation to get acquainted. We have to spend time with them in order to engage with their ideas, mannerisms, behaviors, attitudes, persona, etc. Two of the most important relationships that we have in life are with our God and ourselves. Do you agree? Do you enjoy spending time alone with yourself or with God?

What I have found is that many people are uncomfortable being alone. People are not comfortable going to a new cafe alone, to the movies, for a walk in the park or to musical. I understand that some things are better experienced with others, but what about spending time alone? Riding long distances in the car with no music, going to sleep without the television on, or waking up in the morning with a prayer and journaling? These are just a few things that we can do to get used to time alone.

While we get used to spending time alone, discovering who we are and what gives us energy in life, we can also delve into the Bible to read God's Word. Reading the Bible is a great way to get to know who He is, His ways of doing things and will help us to understand Him while learning about ourselves at the same time. We are created in His image and we have commonalities with Him. He is the Creator, the God of life. He is knowledgeable and intelligent with a great sense of humor. We are extensions of God, like tree trunks and branches. We are connected to Him. That is foundational.

Family of Origin

From the mind of God, we come into the world through parents into a family unit. This family, either directly or indirectly, impacts how the seeds that God planted inside of us are nurtured and how our nature develops. It shapes the way we manage our daily lives, the way we see things, our attitudes and beliefs. Within a family unit, everyone's perception of the common, shared experiences can differ. My brother can talk about a common family experience in one way while his twin sister will express it differently. The middle child will give a different perspective. That is part of the beauty of difference. Harmony does not exist without differences.

Culture

As we come to learn more of ourselves, authentically, we should consider the culture and the role it plays in our identity. Many times, people think of culture as a race, ethnicity or nationality. Although it is true, culture is much more than that. A culture comprises any group of people who share language, values, symbols, and norms. Culture is speech, inside jokes, acceptable behaviors, celebrations, religion, family values, friend groups, sororities and fraternities, colleges and churches. Culture is anywhere you find people. People create culture. A society or nation which represents an entire group of people can create culture. Consider this. America has culture. English is our language. We value freedom, democracy, capitalism and sports, among other things. Our nation is founded on Judeo Christianity. The American flag is a symbol of our nation and is represented by the colors red, white and blue along with 50 stars and 13 stripes.

Within that larger overarching culture, there are co-cultures or smaller groups of people. College students a part of a smaller piece of the larger American culture. There is a culture in academia that is different than corporate American work culture. Those cultures differ from government culture. Cultural values differ from one group to the next based upon the people represented. American culture is represented by African American culture, Asian American culture, American Indian culture, Canadian American culture, French American culture, and German American culture. Culture gets even more narrow as we dial it down. Think about American Veterans. They have a culture of language, experiences, values and norms that the rest of Americans do not have. College students have varied cultural experiences based upon their group affiliation. There is a band culture among colleges. There is a culture amongst Greek members in colleges. And… There is most definitely a PARTY culture on most college campuses. All these groups are part of the American culture but are also a part of these various subcultures.

In addition, your family culture may differ greatly from the culture of the family next door. You may not have ever thought about your family as having a unique culture, but you may. Have you ever heard someone ask the question "Where do they do that??!!" or "Who does that??" The question speaks to cultural differences between people. One group has such strong values on acceptable norms of behavior that differences stick out like a sore thumb. You have your own norms of behavior, values, language, inside jokes, slang, etc. that is used within your family. The values are different. The beliefs are different and so are the ways of being and doing. All this shapes the individual identity.

Because most people are part of multiple cultures, the seeds of our character, abilities, and purpose can be influenced in varied ways. Some family groups (cultures) are more protective of their children and shelter them from external influences. As an adjunct instructor of Communication in Ohio, I have been privileged to serve a very diverse community college student population. My classrooms have taken me around the world, culturally. From 16 yr. old high school students to 60 yr. old nursing students. From Asia, Africa, and France, to the Middle East. From small towns to larger cities, single parents, married couples to divorcees. You name it and I have likely served them in a classroom. Did I mention prisoners? Oh yeah! I have served them too! Why does that matter? Because all of these cultural groups enriched the classroom experience in a way that was transformative for everyone, especially me. Culture plays a part in shaping our perception and worldview. We will a bit talk more about perception later.

American culture is known to be individualistic. This means that, as a whole, our focus is on the individual more than the collective whole. It's about us being our best and putting everything we have out there as we compete for first place. We have the attitude that suggests our ideas and ways of being are most suitable for everyone. Americans are litigious and have an affinity for argument. We will go to court about ANYTHING!

Judge Judy Sheindlin, Judge Marilyn Milian, Judge Greg Mathis, Judge Lynn Toler, and Judge Lauren Lake, for example, keep us engaged, entertained and learning how to effectively live together in peace, solve problems and prepare for court (on TV that is). We believe that your word is your bond. If you say it, you mean it to be final. Have you heard the statement "Those are fighting words!"? Because words carry so much weight and we are litigious in our problem solving, we believe that if it is not written, no one can be responsible for it. In schools, we have syllabi. Human resource departments have onboarding documents. Sales advertisements have fine print. All the contracts, agreements, text messages, and emails are proof of everything. Our nation's constitution delineates our values and the laws that govern us. These things influence our attitudes, behaviors, and worldview.

Some other cultures are more collectivist. They are less concerned about what people say and more focused on behaviors: nonverbal communication. Although collectivists hear the words spoken, the focus is primarily on how the words are expressed. Actions speak louder than words. Thus, these cultures consider body movements and positioning, shifting of eyes, tone of voice, and other behaviors to interpret the meaning of messages. They have a goal of preserving the image of the whole group, thus they address issues and concerns in private, rather than publicly.

Do you remember the movie Akeelah and the Bee? In the movie, Akeelah, an African American student, was in the final round of the spelling bee competition with another student, Dylan. Dylan was Asian, from a collectivist culture. At the competition, Dylan's father pulled him into a private space and harshly expressed his expectations of his son's performance. Akeelah heard him as she walked by. Even though she wanted to win and very well could, she felt bad for Dylan and was embarrassed for what his father said and his expectations of him. As a result, she attempted to shrink her efforts and make intentional errors so that Dylan could win and save face for his father. Their cultural differences were instrumental in how they played the game and ended the competition. This is an example of how culture shapes our perceptions, relations and behaviors.

Personal Preferences

Although we have differences, let's be clear that we are just as much alike as we are different. God created us with varied likes and dislikes. Every person has unique preferences. Sweet, spicy, salty or a combination. Bright, vibrant colors as opposed to pastels. Romantic comedies, sci-fi, dramas, foreign films or documentaries. City living, suburban living, country living or rural living. Laffy Taffy and Now & Laters, Snicker and Almond Joy, or Sugar Free mints. What speaks to you, attracts you, gives you energy, life and brings out your passion, may differ from others. You may be an introvert, an extrovert or ambivert which impacts how you interact with people socially and with yourself. It's all relative to the truth that we were fearfully and wonderfully made, according to Psalm 139:14. This is what makes the world such a magnificent kaleidoscope of colorful, creative, passionate people.

What makes you move and flow with ease and grace, as you do? What motivates you or intimidates you? What causes you to be afraid or gives you pause?

Values

Values are attitudes that one carries to determine the level of importance some things have. We esteem things more or less highly based upon our values. Our core values are those that44we hold close and rarely change. Actually, our values are the guiding light to our philosophy of life. They subconsciously dictate our modus operandi (M.O.). We believe in our values and they are core to who we are. Some values that people have are freedom, independence, honesty, integrity, privacy, dependability, commitment, autonomy, etc. If you are a person who values honesty, you likely have minimal tolerance for liars. Especially not in your intimate circle. Some people have a high tolerance and are forgiving and extend grace to people who make mistakes. Others may not show as much grace and operate from a higher place of excellence and expectations.

All these differences are part of our authentic identity. They impact the things we are attracted to, influence our perception and the direction of our lives. Some of our deepest, often unspoken desires, come out of these places of authenticity. We must be true to ourselves and seek to embody our authenticity! Nothing else will fulfill us, nor those whom we love and serve daily, in the way that being authentic does. Nothing! ***So, Girl, get yo' life!***

When I was a young girl, I wanted to be a wife and have a good marriage with my spouse. That was all that I knew and had seen. My parents were married for 54 years and several of my siblings were married with families. I'm sure that those family values and environment influenced that seed within me to grow and develop. It shaped who I am, my perspective on life and relationships. The question that I did not have the answer to was how to attain a healthy marriage and family? What I have learned is that it all begins with us! ***Girl, get yo' life!***

GIRL, GET YO' LIFE!

4 QUALIFY YOUR CIRCLE

Blessed is the man who walks not in the counsel of the ungodly, nor stands in the way of sinners, nor sits in the seat of the scornful.

- Psalm 1

Meet Kyra, a girl whose mother and family have always affirmed her beauty, intelligence, and creativity. Because Kyra consistently heard from her mother that she was beautiful, intelligent and creative, she believed it to be true and embraced it as part of her identity. There was no other frame of reference for her to negate this preset. She believed what her mother and family members said.

In middle school, Kyra befriended Aria, an equally beautiful and intelligent girl as Kyra. However, Aria did not believe that she was intelligent because although her father affirmed her beauty, he often followed up by telling her she was not smart enough to be anything other than a whore and a baby maker. Kyra often felt terrible for her friend because she could see that Aria was smart and creative like she was, but Aria did not believe it. Regardless of how well she performed in school, she internalized the messages that her father imparted to her, just as Kyra internalized the messages from her mother.

And then there is Monet, a sharp, student-athlete whose parents never affirmed her. They expressed neither their pride nor disappointment in her. They were emotionally detached. Although other people complimented her and offered support, they couldn't penetrate the internalized messages of devalue she felt from her parents.

Many things affect how our self-image is developed. One that I want to spend a little time on here is the concept of reflected appraisal. Reflected appraisal suggests that we often embrace the ideas and perceptions that others have of us. We do so, not only based upon what is spoken verbally, but also from nonverbal or unspoken messages-the way they treat us.

Now, reflected appraisal does not apply to everyone in our lives. It is relative to significant people like our parents, spouses, coaches, teachers, pastors, close friends and even children. The people who are closest to us have a powerful impact on our overall self-concept and who we become. Even though another person's perception may have positive or negative implications for us, be empowered in knowing you have both the right and the responsibility to establish boundaries within your relationship life. As adults, we are in full control of who we allow to speak into and influence our lives. ***Guard yourself, Girl!***

The more that you know and understand about yourself, what compliments you and makes you feel loved, nurtured and empowered, the better able you are to set clear boundaries. It is essential for us to be clear about this because if you don't understand how others influence who you are and how you manage your life, you may end up allowing ANYONE to do ANYTHING in YOUR life. Girl, No! Get Yo' Life! It's yours, not theirs.

But… please be aware that there are people who will GLADLY run your life and tell you who you are and what you should do with your WHOLE life based upon their own agenda. It will not likely be for your best interest. I encourage you to Live Freely!

This is another reason that we must be careful about who we allow in our inner circle. Not only because of the effect of reflected appraisal but also because it is human nature for us to mirror one another's behaviors. Have you heard the idea that you become like the 5 people you spend the most time with? That is your inner circle.

Be selective about who you allow in your space. Take an assessment of your crew. Are they all broke, busted and disgusted? Are they tired of being tired? Are they go-getters moving up the proverbial ladder of success? Are they wealth conscious, visionaries whose focus is long term? Consider this, if 4/5 of them are broke, then you might be well on your way to the same. If they 3/5 are wealth conscious, be careful of the direction that you are pulled. Depending on the influence of the two non-wealth conscious friends, you could move towards wealth or poverty.

In addition, we need to note this because, as women, we often find ourselves in intimate relationships with abusive partners. Around the globe, from coast to coast and from age to age, women have been ostracized, devalued and abused. No matter what type of abuse it is, the impact on our identity and self-worth can be equally detrimental. Physical, emotional, sexual, verbal, financial, and mental abuse are each destructive. Abuse is abuse. Tragically, some women do not recover from their abuse. When I say recover, I mean getting back to themselves, authentically.

Often, an abuser will make many negative claims about you as an individual and about your character. These negative words directed at you, intending to degrade your character reflects the negative self-concept of the abuser. However, even though you may not respond to it immediately, if you're not intentional about rejecting those ideas, you may embrace them as part of your identity. One of my favorite books declares the scripture, "As a man thinks in his heart, so is he in the world." If you accept and embrace those words and ideas, consciously or subconsciously, they will affect who you are and become your identity.

We can reject what people say about us that is untrue or that we do not ascribe to. We don't have to accept the thoughts that come to our minds about ourselves or others, for that matter. It's our choice to address those thoughts and not to embrace them, but to reject them disallowing any direct impact on our self-concept. ***Guard yourself and Get Yo' Life, Sis!***

GIRL, GET YO' LIFE!

5 YOUR TRUE SELF, REPRESENTATIVE OR IMPOSTER

We all have a social mask, right? We put it on, we go out, put our best foot forward, our best image. But behind that social mask is a personal truth, what we really, really believe about who we are and what we're capable of.
- *Dr. Phil McGraw*

As we come to understand more about our identity, the balancing act that we engage with is how to present ourselves, and all that we know about ourselves, to everyone else. When we discover that there are things about us that we don't want other people to know or things about us that are underdeveloped and not ready to be disclosed, we have to balance it. This balancing act is how we manage our image. Our image is our representative.

There are three parts of ourselves that we can introduce people to: our true self, our representative, or the imposter. The true self is the most authentic part of us. It is our core beliefs, values, and expression of authenticity. Our image is the part of us that we want others to see, perceive or engage with. The imposter is neither of those. It is the fake person you present. The imposter neglects anything relative to the true person. It behaves like and looks like someone or something else. It is the most inauthentic, ingenuine of the three.

In the introduction, I posed the question "Who will you introduce when you show up to meet someone?" If you had an opportunity to meet Oprah, who would you want her to meet? Or imagine you have an occasion to meet Former United States President Barack and Michelle Obama. Who do you want them to meet? When you go and meet your boyfriend or girlfriend's family, who do you want them to meet? As you prepare for your final interview for a career opportunity of a lifetime, who will you introduce? Of all that you have discovered of yourself on the journey of self-awareness, what parts of you will you present? We each are challenged to answer these questions. No one is exempt from managing the image. We all do it.

In Hamlet, by William Shakespeare, Polonius said:

> "This above all: to thine own self be true, And it must follow, as the night the day, Thou canst not then be false to any man."

If we are not true to ourselves, then our image/representative will also be untrue, to those whom we meet.

We must not be naïve to think that people will always be honest and open about themselves when we meet. Just as we are managing our image, others are too! Have you ever thought to yourself that while you are on social media, you never want to display your weaknesses or flaws? Is your wall loaded with your best, most funny images and videos of yourself? Do you use those amazing filters on your posts? What is the goal in doing that? Besides the fact that it's cute and makes you look amazing, even with puppy dog ears or bunny nose, does it do anything for you? Sure! It presents you well. Your image is your message to the world. It is the message that you want to send to the world about who you are.

Every single day, we decide, as we meet new people and are in new situations, what we want others to know about us & how we want them to perceive us, whether it be online or face to face. When we think about famous, well known people, entertainers, athletes, high-profile attorneys, police chiefs, presidents, CEOs, and other C-Suite professionals, we must remember that they have a responsibility to maintain the image that has been established for them. If they represent themselves, a company, or brand, we, as consumers, have to decipher that and do our best not to confuse the true person with the representative (image). The difficulty in doing this is that it is human nature for us to connect with people whom we admire or feel connected to in some way.

When we watch movies and TV shows, we can feel as though we know these people. We cry with them. We laugh with them, at their experiences. We relate intimately with them. The question is, is it the true person, their representative or an imposter? Clearly, if it is a TV character, they represent a character, not themselves. Although, there are times when an actor/actress will express in an interview that their personality is very similar to a character they play.

Beyoncé, for example, is a brand. There is an image that goes along with the brand. Because we have fallen in love with and bought into the Beehive image and the brand, we continue to buy into everything Beyoncé. We love her music and her presence as an entertainer; therefore, she can drop 3 albums in one day, while in concert on tour; each one will be multi-platinum! They average person, however, cannot do anything like that because they don't have the image and brand recognition or notoriety that is known and bought into like Beyoncé.

When you hear that Gary Owen is going to be in concert, you buy your tickets. Why? Because you have fallen in love with the brand, the image, what he represents and his comedic ability. The fact of the matter is the images that we see on television, in movies, and on social media are often not true to the identity of the individual. The image is a representation of what the marketer's, advertisers and producers want consumers to buy into. When I have seen an interview with Beyoncé, she can be quite soft-spoken, appear somewhat timid and a bit shy. Do you agree? But onstage, she is totally different. When she is performing, you don't see any of that! She is Sasha Fierce! And fierce she is!

Here is a tip to help you make good decisions as you engage with people online. When you meet someone, you don't know which of the three parts of themselves they are introducing to you, nor do you know what their motivation is. There are A LOT of hidden agendas and imposters online and on social media. Don't be catfished! Be vigilant in guarding yourself against opportunists seeking to manipulate you online. It becomes a bit more challenging to decipher the authentic, representative and imposter online. Who's hiding behind the screen? I just gave you the advantage. You are at least clearer and more aware of what awaits you on social media. ***Girl, Get Yo Life!***

GIRL, GET YO' LIFE!

6 YOU ARE NOT AN ACCIDENT

"The two most important days in your life are the day you are born and the day you find out why."
-Mark Twain

According to www.history.com., the World Trade Center was purposed to facilitate world peace through trade. In 1973, they completed the Twin Towers. The buildings were the tallest skyscrapers in the world and each was 110 stories high, with at least 200,000 guests each day and 50,000 employees. They were massive steel and glass structures with a foundation of at least 70 feet deep. The elevators carried 97 people and up to 10,000 lbs. Altogether, there were 40,000 doors, 43,600 windows, six acres of marble, 3,000 miles of electrical wiring and 425,000 cubic yds of concrete. Whew!

The engineers and architects planned these buildings to withstand massive amounts of weight, both internally and externally. The depth and fortitude of the foundation was a critical part of how well the building maintained itself for so many years. There were very detailed materials, characteristics of the buildings, time to develop, and specifications critical to the Twin Towers of the World Trade Center. They knew EVERYTHING that the buildings could withstand. The only thing that was not considered was a terrorist attack. That was the one thing that destroyed the structures after 28 years.

Somewhere deep inside, we believe that our lives have a purpose. We may wonder, from time to time what to do with our lives, to get it on the right path and "together", as we say. However, these ideas can be ephemeral. Be encouraged in knowing that even more masterfully and wonderfully than those detailed skyscrapers, is your unique design and purpose.

Our life mission is how we use our gifts, passions, knowledge, and experiences to serve others in our circle of influence and beyond. Many people know that they have a purpose, but they don't understand how to discover it. In addition, some don't understand how our identity correlates to our mission.

As we wonder or ask what on earth are we here for, consider that the more primary question is "who am I?" The reason is that there is a direct correlation between who we are and what we do, which is our purpose. If I were to ask you "who are you?" or ask you to tell me a little about yourself, what would you say? Many times, our first responses are the roles we play. We might say I am a mother, sister, brother, husband, wife, student, boss, or employer. These are truly roles we play; however, they don't describe who we are. It's important for us to differentiate the roles we play and who we are.

This is significant because who we are leads to the roles we play and our purpose. I believe that this is one reason that many are unsure of their life purpose. How can we know what our purpose is and what we are called to do aside from knowing and embracing ourselves intimately? Apart from our inner voice or the voice of God, how can we know?

Being introspective and self-aware gives us more understanding of ourselves in a way that empowers us in every area of our lives. We learn more about ourselves from interactions with others. Who we are, the characteristics we possess, those unique interests and things about us that stand out, are clues to our purpose. We often get consumed with where, to whom or in what capacity we should serve in our purpose. However, our priority should be to discover our defining treasures within and what we can do with them. The bottom line is that who we are influences the roles we play in life. Roles don't determine who we are. We play and perform roles and they influence our assignment.

The Assignment

Based on who we are and the roles we play, our assignment has been prepared for us. As we journey through life, we find that we are drawn to certain characteristics in people, situations, and industries that are clues to our purpose. You may have heard it said before that the things we experience in life are not about us. As we go through difficult situations, it doesn't feel good to hear those words because it feels like, and in some ways, it is about us, however; I don't believe it's primarily about us. But it is about others. Because we were created for fellowship with one another, we know that the things we experience in life either benefit or are disadvantageous to those in our circles. Our lives are not our own. It was a gift given to us to share. Life is about purpose and assignment and those who we are connected to in our families, schools, churches, workplaces, communities and in the world. Everyone is not meant to have a global impact or a big and fancy lifestyle, like social media and reality TV, depicts.

However, we are to serve one another. We cannot healthily journey through this life experience alone. We need one another. Although everyone is not to make a global impact, everyone impacts make in the grand cycle of life. One water's, one plant's, and God brings forth the increase, it is said. We may be the planter. We may be the one to water. We may be the cultivator. We may be the tiller. Or we may be the pruner. To impact others around us is our assignment.

When I was 9 years old, my grandmother passed

away. Although I did not have many memories of her, she was still my only living grandparent. On her passing, a neighbor down the street offered to be my grandmother. She heard me. She taught me. She supported me. She shared her life and her wisdom with me. For that, I am grateful. She was a planter in my life.

Ofttimes, I have met a young woman or young man seeking wisdom, guidance or perspective on a life issue. In the most honest and ethical way possible, I took it upon myself to offer support, encouragement, guidance, wisdom, nurturing, hugs, and love to those young people. I did so because I recognize the value of having support in our lives. I also recognize how detrimental it can be not having it. Misinformation is almost as bad as no information at all. If you have ever been misinformed or misdirected, then you understand what it's like to be running 100 miles per hour towards a goal, only to find out you are going the wrong direction. It can be devastating and so discouraging.

Our life's mission it's a serve one another, that we may continue to grow in a healthy life cycle. Every goal is to help others become the best version of themselves that they can be. And as they do so, we too grow to become the best versions of ourselves. One cannot support and influence others without impacting her own soul, her own heart, her own life. Our assignment has been prepared for us based upon the course of life we are to take and the characteristics we possess. Remember, we are built, designed by a creative, purposeful God.

Remember the Twin Towers from earlier? We too are built for what we are purposed to do. There is no question whether we have the capacity to withhold and to stabilize in situations that call for our innate creativity, gifting, passions, preferences, and genius. We have absolutely everything that we need to fulfill the assignment and do what we are designed to. Whether it be to motivate, to support, to encourage, to teach, to train, to serve, to lead, to administer, to develop, to create, or to build.

We have the capacity to do it. We are created with everything we need. It is already inside of us, to be cultivated, discovered and strengthened to grow. If it is true that our gifts make room for us and opens doors for us, then a person can be trained to do certain things, however, those who are gifted and innately possess the characteristics required to perform that task, role or job, will do it with ease and Grace. No training necessary. As my coach, Mia Redrick, The Mom Strategist says, "it is as if you are breathing". We don't need skill or training to breathe. No education required. Just breathing, the way we are created to.

Have you ever seen a building or house that has been abandoned for years? The windows are burst out. There are weeds and ivy as high as the front door. The ground is unlevel and cracked because of unkept tree roots growing beneath it. Bricks are missing from the building and there is graffiti on it. The inside of the house is wrecked, much like the outside, except that there is mold throughout, decayed wood floors and missing copper pipes.
Not to mention, there is an invasion of rats, mice, and termites. If I were to look at that house with my eye and my purpose, I would think it was irreparable and need to be demolished because for me it looks wrecked already. Yet, a person who is a creative visionary with an eye for restoring structures will probably look at that building and see the beauty at a foundational level. They can visualize the building restored before it even gets close to a written blueprint. That's his assignment. This person has the capacity, vision, skills, and gifts needed to fulfill the purpose in that building. That is the assignment.

In an interview, Coretta Scott King, the late wife of the late Dr. Martin Luther King Jr., Bishop TD Jakes asked her what her life purpose was. She responded that it was to serve as Dr. King's wife. She never took another husband. She never served another purpose. That was her purpose until the day she died. She fulfilled the role with eloquence, grace, wisdom, and strength of character. If someone else had been in the role of his wife, the Civil Rights Movement, as we know it, would not have been the same. It may not have been as successful as it was. Why do you say that, Ms. Lawson? Because it takes a special woman to raise children, pray for her husband whose life was sought after by unknown heartless people to assassinate and maintain peace. What kind of home do you think a man under the pressure that Dr. King was, needs to come home to? There is no place for insecurity. There is no place for nagging. There is no place for abuse. There is no place for any of that drama. She was Dr. King's wife, his girdle, his supporter, his backbone. When he stood, she stood behind him and undergirded him in prayer and nurtured his children. Wherever she went, she always carried his name and his purpose in her heart and never let it die. When they met and married, neither of them knew that he was called to the movement. However, both were equipped to serve in their assignments. That's powerful and encouraging, isn't it? Do you believe it?

Every place we go, we are on assignment. That assignment is to serve others in how we are created and gifted to do so. That is the assignment. Count it a joy whenever we serve, at our highest level, the people who we are assigned to impact, transform and support. It is a privilege that every person represents a part of a whole. It's bigger than us and NOT about us.

A Symphony Orchestra is composed of a variety of instruments including woodwinds, percussion, brass, and strings. Each of them plays a different note, within the same key, to create a beautiful masterpiece of music. Do they all have the same sound? No, they do not. They play their individual parts together, in the same key and all their variations create the beautiful harmonized masterpiece we call music and song.

Such is life. We are all a part of an Orchestra of sorts—the cycle of life. Each instrument has a different sound and at its appointed time, will create harmony with the others in song. Discover the beauty of who you are, the innate sound you make, as if you are breathing, and play it in the orchestra of life. You will create an empowering, transformative impact in yourself, your family, community, church, school, and beyond.

You are the answer to someone's question. You are the solution to someone's problem. You are the answer to a prayer cried in the night's silence. You are assigned to impact and influence others. Won't you serve today? Will your life have a greater meaning? Will you keep it all for yourself? Will it be in vain? No. Everyone has a story, but it doesn't read the same because of our fingerprint, our impact, our reflection, our influence, is woven into the story. ***Girl, Get Yo' Life, so you can give it away!***

7 YOUR PERCEPTION IS *YOUR* REALITY

As a man thinks in his heart, so is he in the world. (Proverbs 27:19)
- Holy Bible

Perception affects every area of our interactions. What is perception exactly? Perception is the process of making meaning of the things we experience in our environment. It is the mental gymnastics we go through to get an understanding of what is happening around us. It is our way of seeing the world. It is the lens through which you see, understand and make sense of your physical surroundings and your interactions with others. Perception affects the way that we see ourselves, other people, behaviors, and conflicts. It can even influence the way you see and receive love and attention.

To relate well to others and to have good people skills, we must understand that perceptions are as unique as we are. Let's say that you wear contact lenses. The prescription is specific to you. It's requirements don't match mine. Therefore, if I were to put your contacts on and look around, I'll see everything much differently than you do.

Perceptions are shaped by YOUR experiences, beliefs, core values, and knowledge. There may be 25 students in a classroom listening to a lecture and EACH will go away from that interaction with a different idea, experience and emotion that was evoked. One may laugh, one quietly shaken, one in tears and yet another untouched. Perception influences all these differences. In the current information driven society, we are constantly bombarded with messages to decipher. Each having to travel through our individual perceptual filters, just as water from pasta drains through a colander.

As communicators, it is our aim and responsibility to help others understand our perspective. Because they cannot see through our "prescription lenses", we must consider the lens they see through and help them make sense of the message. Your experiences can shape that.

Here's a scenario. Let's say that you are sitting in the lounge on campus with two of your friends and you see a guy and girl walk in. She appears to be upset. He is walking behind her toward the vending machine for coffee. There are tears in her eyes. Once they get their drinks, they find seats in a secluded corner. The three of you at the table may perceive the situation differently, based upon your filter (prescription lenses). Brittney grew up in an abusive family environment. She would recognize the expression on the girl's face and identify that the guy has hurt or threatened her. Tre' has had family members who have experienced traumatic health crises, and he recognized the girl hurting as his aunt did when she learned that she has stage 4 metastatic breast cancer. In his perception, she was clearly devastated. Now, Nicole was so fixated on her new Boo and their romance, that she only thought the pair may have had a little spat, as people often do. The fact remains that neither of them knew what was going on in the situation, but they each perceived something based upon their individual filters.

One main way this supports us as we pursue better, more effective and healthy communication interactions is that we are empowered in knowing that our "prescription lens" differs from someone else's. Although they may understand from your position, likely they have their own view. The goal is to help them perceive what we do in the unique way we do it. This information helps us to better understand the people interact with daily. Instead of trying to change people, we can embrace others for the value that they bring to the table, which is their difference. ***Girl, Get Yo' Life and let others get theirs!***

8 SPEAK LOVE TO ME

If love is a verb, expressed in word and deed, then say and do things that speak love to me.
-Rachelle Lawson

Are you familiar with the Dr. Seuss children's book entitled <u>Are You My Mother?</u> In the story, a mother bird was nesting with her egg in a tree. When she went away to get food, the egg hatched, and the baby bird was born. The baby bird looked all around for his mother, from the nest in the tree until he jumped to the ground and searched for her. Although he had never seen his mother, there was a part of him that longed for her. She had kept him warm and safe his entire incubation period and now he was born; he yearned for her. He was relentless in his quest to find her. Baby bird inquired of every "thing" that he came across. Nothing was excluded in his search. From other animals to trucks, he searched until he found his mother, to fulfill his innate longing.

We are much like that baby bird with the need and longing for love. When we are born into the world, we may or may not get the attention, affection, nurturing and touch we yearn. Whether consciously or not, as humans, we seek to fill the need for love in people and things. In our effort to satisfy the innate longing for agape love, we try food, material things, attention for external sources of power or fame and most especially relationships. With no frame of reference, how do we know when we are loved? It is one of the deepest and most natural questions we ask.

One body of research I support is the theory of Love Languages by Dr. Gary Chapman. He is a world-renowned scholar who developed this body of research that has had positive impacts on myriad relationship types including single adults, parent-child, marriages, employee-manager, etc. It applies to all relationships, as it is interpersonal. The message is simple, yet profound.

Language is a symbol, created by those who use it, to communicate messages. It does not matter whether you use words, sounds, nonverbal cues or silence, we are ALWAYS communicating a message. Regardless of your intention, it is impossible not to communicate a message to another person. It is the nature of human communication.

Dr. Chapman suggests that there are 5 languages that communicate love and we, as humans, respond to them. We express the 5 Love Languages to others through both words and behaviors that facilitate one feeling loved. The 5 Love Languages are:

1. Words of Affirmation

2. Quality Time

3. Acts of Service

4. Physical Touch

5.   Receiving Gifts

You might ask me, why are you telling me this, Ms. Lawson? Because your relationships can be strengthened by tapping into what makes you feel loved, valued, appreciated and supported.

Allow me to introduce you to a couple. Ashley and Jaylen are engaged to be married. During their premarital counseling, they discovered their love languages. Ashley's primary love language is acts of service. Jaylen's primary love language is quality time. Understanding this, Jaylen always does things for Ashley. He washes her car and keeps it detailed every few weeks and he prepares dinner for her at least three nights each week. She loves it and feels especially cared for.

Ashley is not as intentional about spending time with Jaylen. She does things for him too! Being a talented writer, she edits all his written projects for school and organizes his bill payments. Although Jaylen appreciates what she does for him, he often complains that they rarely spend time together. Does he feel loved by Ashley? Yes, he may, but only to a degree. He may feel a measure of love because he understands that doing things for people expresses love and generosity. However, he would feel more loved if they spent quality time together. Learning this early in the relationship is vital to the success of the marriage. I find many of the issues that bring couples to divorce in the love language.

What could Ashley do to spend time with Jaylen? She could invite him to be with her while she edits his work or while she organizes his bills. She could also help him while he cleans her car. Those are just two ways she can include him in what she is already doing "for" him and do them "with" him. It's natural to do, but we have to be intentional about speaking love to those we care about, once we learn what makes another person feel loved. Speak love to your friends, your children, your parents, your partner, your business associates, etc. It is a great way to let people know that you take an interest in their lives and care about them. As opposed to treating them as though they are just like everyone else. We are rare and worthy of being known intimately and genuinely cared for.

This is part of the reason I devoted an entire chapter to identity. It's critical to know that about yourself so you can give what others need, but also so you can get *your* needs met. It's so valuable.

A few years ago, I had one student in his early 20s who was struggling in a relationship with his parents, particularly with his father. They were close to one another, but they had become distanced from each other. I introduced the class to the Five Love Languages and encouraged interested students to take the test. I took a copy of the book to class. When this young man read the book and implemented what he discovered and what he believed to be his father's love language. He was right! It shifted the direction of the relationship. Isn't that wonderful?

When I was about 14 years old, I remember asking my father, "Daddy, do you love me?" My family was intact with my father in the home. His response was "Of course I love you, Baby! Why do you ask me that?" I replied, "When will you tell me? when I die?" I appreciated that conversation with my father. I was crying out to my father to speak my language, but it came out that way. My parents provided everything. I traveled with the band, ate McDonald's Big Macs with my cousins, had candy and money when I asked for it. I could go to many places. My parents provided those things, but for me, that did not mean I FELT loved.

Even though he was present, gave me all I needed and wanted and spoiled me, as an adolescent, I didn't feel particularly loved by him. Why? What I realized later in life was that I was asking this question out of my love language. I was starving for him to tell me, affirm me. Although he showed me in other ways, what I felt most was a lack of my love language being spoken. Had he affirmed me more, I would have had a better sense of self and been a more confident young adult. I would have *known*, from my perspective, that my father loved me.

If you have observed people for any length of time, then you have seen or heard about a young girl searching for love, especially from a father. When people in her close circle don't speak her language, where can she get that from? This vulnerability can open her up to receive from anyone or anything. It could be the first boy, man, girl or woman she meets who speaks her love language. That can either be helpful or disadvantageous to this young girl.

Why is that important in relationships? If we tell others "I love you", do things for them, buy flowers, wash their car, clean the garage, take them to the movie on the weekends or out for dinner once a month, shouldn't that be enough? We do things to show love, tell them they are loved, buy gifts that show love, etc. If it doesn't make them feel loved, then is it love for them? On some level it is, but not deeply.

We speak the language of love we need. If my language is acts of service, I would do things for others to show my love. If their love language is not acts of service, they do not need the acts of service to feel loved. If it is our responsibility in a relationship to convey love, then we need to know what that is, not only for the other person but for ourselves. When you take the quiz for yourself and determine what your language of love is you will better be able to maintain healthy relationships with those you care about.

You must be deliberate to assure them that you love them. It is selfish to assume that because YOU think you show them love or because YOU know that you love someone, that they also feel and know the same. Be intentional. Don't be lazy with relationships. It doesn't matter if I tell them every night before bed, show up to their games or concerts every time, or give them gifts for every occasion or no occasion. Those things are the icing on the cake to speaking love to them.

Go to www.5lovelanguages.com to take the quiz online and determine your primary and secondary love languages. Then you can behave more intentionally with those you care about. ***Girl, Get Yo' Love Life!***

9 STICKS, STONES AND WORDS THAT HURT

Death and Life are in the power of the tongue… Proverbs 18:21a KJV

In a world riddled by violence, many people have become desensitized to abuse and abusive language. We saw variations of abuse in the movie *The Burning Bed* starring Farrah Fawcett. We also read about it in the novel *Push* by Sapphire and in *Finding Fish: A Memoir* by Antwone Quenton Fisher, among others. When these two stories became movies, *Precious* and *The Antwone Fisher Story*, respectively, we were shown the tragedy and cycles of abuse as they unfolded and were subsequently broken.

Although physical and sexual abuse are the most widely known types of abuse, there are others, such as verbal abuse, financial abuse, mental abuse, and digital abuse. According to the National Domestic Violence Hotline, domestic violence and abuse are defined as a pattern of behaviors used by one partner to maintain power and control over another partner in an intimate relationship. Regardless of the abuse, the fact remains - it's all very painful. The late Dr. Myles Munroe defined abuse as "the abnormal use of something or someone." He also said, "If you don't know the purpose of something, then you will abuse it or abnormally use it".

Irrespective of the abuse, it's unhealthy in relationships. If you grew up in a family where abuse was normal, it becomes challenging for you as an adult to understand the difference between normal and abnormal behavior or expressions of love, care and comfort because it's unfamiliar to you. When we don't know our purpose, we may abuse ourselves or allow other people to abuse or mistreat us.

What is difficult is that growing up in a family where abuse was present, one often grows up, moves out and dates or marries someone who behaves similarly to what they are used to. It's familiar; and not knowing or recognizing the signs of abuse, one is more likely to enter that same type of relationship: abusive. It's like jumping from the frying pan into the fire. Both are burning hot. Do you see the cycle forming? Children who come out of these relationships will probably have similar experiences. The ultimate tragedy is that some people don't make it out of abusive relationships alive. It is detrimental and traumatic for everyone involved.

Let's unmask signs of abuse. As stated in the definition, the goal of an abuser is to gain and maintain power and control over another person. They do so by using abusive language and/or behavior to exert power and control. I want to expose some of these signs to make us aware and able to make better choices when we see them early on. Red flags are always waving, and the writing is always on the wall, but if we don't know what to look for then we can misinterpret what we see. Some signs of abuse in relationships are:

- isolation from friends and family
- taking money from you or forcing you to put all the bills in your name

- looking at you in an intimidating way
- extreme jealousy
- destruction of property, animals, and things that can hurt you
- intimidation with weapons
- pressure and forced to use drugs or alcohol
- poking holes in a condom or secretly taking it off
- coercion to give your passwords to social media, cell phones, and computer
- making you give them your tax return or taking your joint return, forbidding you to work
- purposely and knowingly passing a sexually transmitted disease to you
- sending mean, negative and insulting emails and texts
- checking your phone and social media accounts
- manipulation and control of where you go, how long you stay and what you wear
- demanding or forcing sex when you refuse, are sick, and after hurting you

- insults, degrading language, cursing, and put-downs (even if it's meant jokingly)

- threats against you, your children or family of taking children away

Many people experience abusive environments where it is normalized. Thus, it all looks and feels the same. These experiences shape our perceptions which are real for us. Our perception affects how we move about in life and relationships with others. (more on perception later) We must understand that what is normal and consistent behavior in our household is not necessarily normal and consistent in others' homes.

It is important to talk about and show our children the difference between pure love and abuse. In order for us to do so, we must recognize, understand and heal from our experiences and create change for future generations. The values that used to hold families together are not as prevalent as they once were. They still exist, but they are not as strong.

One example of this is family mealtime at the dinner table. This single habit is one the central forces of togetherness for families. At the table, families share their experiences of the day, new knowledge and ideas learned, expectations of behavior, laughter, frustration, love and attention. Those 30-60 minutes of daily time together for a family is critical to the lives of those seated around it. It is a time to connect, reflect, teach, model and learn from one another. The intimacy of the family table can also increase the self-value one feels. Children often feel more loved, valued and appreciated when sharing time together with family at the dinner table. Parents have the ability to look into the eyes of their children and see if they are hiding, lying about something, high on drugs or otherwise detached.

In a study published by Psychology Today, researchers found that adolescents who shared a meal at the table with their families 5-7 times weekly, were less likely to engage in risky behaviors like drug use, violence, antisocial behavior, depression-suicide and alcohol abuse. Also, the study shows that young people are less likely to steal, destroy property, from home or exhibit physical violence.

With the increase in technology and social media, the need to detach from devices and engage in face to face interactions is ever more necessary. The pressures of perfection and image management in our current culture is literally killing our children, especially those who do not interact and engage in these family social traditions of togetherness.

Signs of Abuse

Signs of abuse exist on a spectrum from subtle teasing and put-downs to more violent, threatening signs like intimidation and rape. Some signs of abuse have greater danger associated with them. One is high levels of jealousy. Jealousy is a secondary emotion that is expressed when one perceives that something they possess or someone they have a relationship with is threatened by another. Secondary emotions are a combination of two or more primary emotions. Primary emotions singular expressions that are easily recognizable across all cultures, peoples and times. The primary emotions are happiness, sadness, fear, anger, surprise, and disgust. Jealousy is a combination of anger and fear, both of which are primary emotions. It could be perceived fear of loss of position in someone's life and anger because the person feels violated. They may feel threatened in their relationship, status in a relationship, or by someone who may have an influence on taking causing the relationship to end.

Meet Kasey and Marc, a young couple who have been dating for several years. Kasey has had no boyfriends other than Marc. However, prior to dating Kasey, Marc had two failed dating relationships. The first girl cheated on him with his friend, right under his nose. The second one broke up with him to be with another girl. How do you think Marc internalized these experiences based on a reflected appraisal we learned in Chapter 3? Marc was likely feeling insecure, angry, bitter, worthless, etc. When he met Kasey, she differed from what he knew of the other girls, but he still had not processed those relationships. He was nice and fun when he was with Kasey. They enjoyed each other's company and had a lot in common. Their personalities complimented each other well, overall. There was one thing, about four months into the relationship, Marc became possessive. He wanted Kasey to spend all her spare time with him. He would become annoyed when she spent, what he perceived as, too much time with her sister and best friend. Kasey was a virgin and was waiting to be married before she had sex. Initially, Marc was accepting of this and was glad about it. But, when his insecurities rose, he became more aggressive in his efforts to get Kasey to have sex. Kasey did not understand what was happening with Marc.

This situation has various red flags. The question is, does Kasey recognize them and know how to respond. If she does, then she has the advantage. For those who don't know or read the language of abuse well, they are at a disadvantage. High levels of jealousy of partners, friends, and family are common. People make statements like, "I don't really have many friends", "I don't need to go anywhere", "He needs me at home", "He doesn't like me to go out", or "She doesn't like me to be out with my friends", etc. Being disconnected from friends, family, and other social networks is isolation. It is not good.

Checking up on your partner constantly is another sign of dangerous abuse. It may flatter you to think they are always thinking about you and really care about you. You may think he wants to be familiar with what you are doing all the time and is taking an interest in your life. Although that may be true at a base level, being able to differentiate between being cared for and being controlled and manipulated is key. It is abuse at that point. It may not always be the case, but it can be.

Controlling who you see, where you go, or who you talk to is a level of abuse. An abuser may ask why you're always talking to a particular person on the phone. It could be your mother, cousin, coworker or friend. This control can stem from jealousy or protection, but we must know the difference. An abuser can only control the person they are in a relationship with. Though they may attempt to control others, they only control those who submit to it.

Another favorite movie of mine is *What's Love Got to Do With It*, starring Angela Bassett and Laurence Fishburne. This movie is a depiction of the life of Ike and Tina Turner. It shows how a woman can empower herself and escape the torment of an abusive relationship. At a diner, Ike offered Tina a piece of cake to celebrate the occasion. Tina wanted none of the cake and refused it. He asked again. She refused a second time. The third time he smashed the cake in her face and told her to eat the cake. Tina's friend and bandmate argued with Ike about it.

As she got up from the table to leave, Tina told her it was all right - everything was all right. Her friend yelled that "it is NOT all right to let someone pound on you!" And she walked out. Ike could not control the friend, but he had Tina controlled in her mind. Everywhere she went, Ike was there. She felt as though she couldn't escape. After a few more incidents, Tina empowered herself, fought Ike back physically, in court and in the subsequent divorce. She won, in the end! The dangerous red flags were waving all around early on, but she did not know how to read them.

Hurting the partner or acts of physical violence is dangerous. Grabbing hard, wrestling, fighting, hitting, punching, stabbing are all acts of violence. While working in a women's prison, I met many students who were serving 25 years to life sentences for killing the men who attempted to sexually abuse their child or hurt them. Many of them stated that they would do it again to protect themselves and their children. What I learned was that many of these women had experienced similar abuse in their childhood, and for one reason or another, their "protector" did not protect them. So, when they killed the abuser, they were not only protecting their child(ren) but also standing up for themselves as a child.

Making people feel small and stupid is another form of abuse, enjoy putting you down. The abuser strips down your beliefs and values. Have you ever heard the saying, "Sticks and stones may break my bones, but words will never hurt me?" This is just as untrue as the tooth fairy and Santa Claus. Bones can heal because God made the body a magnificent self-preserving machine. Words are powerfully impactful because their energy penetrates the soul and mind. They transfer from one to another. They do not fall in a dead place. They take root and grow like all other living things.

Forced sex happens in dating relationships and in marriage. I know that may be hard to believe, but it is true. I know women who experience that. I know that in marriage, your body is not your own. Each spouse belongs to the other spouse.

However, if one is sick, physically or emotionally, and declines sex, the partner should respect the boundary. There is no respect in forced sex. This is another sign of abuse.

Negative words, insults, and demeaning language are cruel. If it makes you feel bad or behave badly, then it is unhealthy and abusive. When others make you feel incompetent and small, even as a joke, it can rip away at your core being. Be careful not to internalize the words. The effects on the self-esteem, confidence and on the image are tremendous. It can hurt for a very long time.

These are signs of abuse. Recognizing the signs early in a relationship can protect us and our children. Be confident, know and embrace yourself as you are. Embody that person before you connect yourself in lifelong, intimate relationships. ***Get yo' life first, Girl!***

10 TO COMPLETE OR TO COMPLIMEMT

Half of a woman and a half of a man don't make a whole marriage like a pie. I need to be a whole individual and you need to be a whole individual to make a whole marriage.
— *Bishop TD Jakes*

As we learned early on, the benefits of knowing yourself are foundational to life. Much of our life hinges on our identity (who you are authentically) and purpose (what you are to do with it). Our uniqueness determines how we add value to our relationships with others and the world. That is the beauty of differences. Our superpower or differentiating factor makes us valuable and attractive to others. The fact that differences and similarities are attractive to us does not determine whether we complete or complement one another.

As an educator, I often advise my students that if someone you are in a relationship with says you complete them, RUN FOR THE BORDER! You never want to be empowered in a position of completing someone.

In life, one of our primary goals is to be whole, complete individuals who impact our families, communities and the world. One definition of wholeness suggests that a person or thing is complete with nothing missing, and nothing broken from it. Your needs are met. You are confident and self-aware with a good understanding of your gifts, calling and position in life. Every day, a complete person is walking in truth and authenticity.

To be complete also is to have an undeniable relationship with God, as you do with your friends and family. You spend time together, reading His Word to learn more about Him and talk to Him in prayer like you talk to your mom and friends and read their text messages. Investing time in others is how we learn of them, connect, bond, get to know, like and trust them. God is His Word, therefore, reading His Word and praying is spending time with Him. As we do so, we get more of our innermost needs met and the gaps and holes in our lives mend. Nobody and nothing can meet this level of completeness. That's the truth. Thus, our goal should be to be whole, complete individuals in Him before we connect our hearts and lives in any hookups, dating or marital relationships.

We should assure that we are joining ourselves with another whole, complete individual. We owe it to ourselves, our families and our futures. The only time that we should choose otherwise is if we have DECIDED that we are investing in a project for the relationship, as opposed to a partner. Ask yourself if you want a partner or a project? Be honest with yourself because YOU must be able to accept whatever you buy-in to. Jim Rohn used to say, "Don't be lazy with language." I say, "Don't be lazy with relationships."

Connecting with others unequally is a setup for disappointment and violation of expectations. Remember, we choose who we allow access to our lives and our hearts. We must be clear about who we are and what we bring to the table or how we add value to others and then CHOOSE our partnerships or projects accordingly. That's what happens when one person is incomplete within themselves and expects the other person to complete them. Be whole and expect wholeness in your partnerships.

To complement is to add to, accompany or supplement something, according to Webster's Dictionary. I like to compare this idea to supplementary and complementary angles from Geometry. Do you remember those? I love geometry and am hopeful I will lose no one because it's math! Think about this. Any degree of an angle is a complete angle. It may be 20°, 40° or 120°. It needs nothing else to make it a whole angle. Something happens when 2 complete angles come together. They form another angle. A 30° angle supplements a 60° angle to form a 90° angle or right angle. Likewise, two 90° right angles complement each other to form a 180° straight line. Right? To add value to the angle they created, the only thing that they needed was to be a complete angle.

In partnerships, it's ideal to join with another who is whole like you, as are the angles. You don't have to be exactly alike, but each must be complete within in order to have a viable partnership. There are two reasons I suggest this. First, it is not your responsibility to make the other whole. Second, we CANNOT make someone whole. We don't have what it takes. our humanness. In our finite knowledge and wisdom, we don't have what it takes. Although we would like to think we do, we don't. Only the creator of the individual has the infinite wisdom, knowledge, and capacity to make and remake what He originally created. We often step outside of our positions to play God in the lives of others and when we fall short or err, we feel terrible. We must learn to stay in our own lane and support one another in our partnerships, as we are able. To be honest, people who are broken themselves may try to complete or fix someone else to help them feel better about their lives. Although it is our duty to serve others when they are weak, it is not the same as being in a partnership with an incomplete person and expect them to glean from your wholeness to make themselves whole.

If we expect another person to make us whole, as soon as the cake falls, the cookies crumble, the milk spills, I make a mistake, have a crisis or a life challenge that causes me not to be my best self, your life falls apart. What? It is unreasonable for anyone to expect this of another person. You must be complete yourself and have a main source and tools to support you. It is self-care; in that, we are empowered to get into a space where you can be refilled or rejuvenated. *Girl, Get Yo' Life!*

I am not, by any means, suggesting that we do not support one another and lean on others we are in a relationship with. That is furthest from the truth. In fact, relationships provide myriad rewards for everyone involved because we bring everything we have and are to them; good, bad and indifferent.

However, we must have balanced expectations and proper perspective of each other. Feeling incomplete is natural when our souls are void meaning and direction. This is where many get into trouble. Not only do they look for their partners, spouses, or friends to complete them and fill the void, many seek material things like shoes, drugs, food, shopping, sex, work, etc. Taking time daily to spend quietly with ourselves, with no interferences, can help us get centered and in tune with our creator. Prayer, meditation, journal writing or just sitting quietly in the moment are excellent self-care practices to support our efforts.

It's possible that people who empower others to complete them are just saying what they have heard as opposed to really believing it to be true. Either way, I hear it too often to assume. The bottom line is that broken people need to heal individually in order to have the best and most positive impact on any relationship. Let broken people heal and practice self-care strategies to manage your expectations about their availability to you as they heal. ***Get yo' life, Girl!***

11 EVERYONE WINS

It is one of the beautiful compensations of life that no man can sincerely try to help another without helping himself.
-Ralph Waldo Emerson

As it is with many interpersonal interactions, our perception plays a tremendous role. Conflict is no different. In every relationship between humans, conflict is inevitable. It doesn't matter if a relationship is between a husband and wife, parents and children, employees and employers, friends, or strangers. There will be a conflict. The reason is that differences are necessary for there to be harmony.

Since we are all unique with varied preferences, conflict and disagreement will occur. Pride comes into play when people believe that who they are, what they know and do are better than others. Interpersonal conflict is an expressed struggle between two interdependent parties who perceive incompatible goals, scarce resources or interference from the other party in achieving their goal. The struggle is expressed either verbally or nonverbally; what you say or how you say it.

These conflicts occur between people who depend on one another in some way. Whether it is a teacher who gives grades, an employer who issues a paycheck, a spouse who cooks dinner, or doctor who prescribes medication, we depend on one another for our needs wherever our lives intersect.

There are four types of conflict we engage in: ego conflict, pseudo-conflict, content and value conflict. Let's talk about them. The most common conflict is an ego conflict. It is a simple personality conflict. It has nothing to do with any issues or behavior. It is solely about the person. Imani walks into the room where you are sitting. She is a self-proclaimed DIVA who is well dressed, confident and captivating. She has not mumbled a single word not done anything to grab attention besides walking into the room. Tamika immediately picks up her bottle of "Hater-Aid" and takes a big sip. She leans over to her girl and spews her criticisms about Imani. Tamika doesn't like her style; the way she carries herself nor her bag. She doesn't like her hair and thinks Imani wears too much makeup. It is a simple conflict over preferences.

A pseudo conflict is when you agree with someone, but you think you disagree. The perceived disagreement can come from a lack of understanding or miscommunication. It can also arise in the heat of an argument or disagreement when listening skills are out the window! Do you know what I mean? That moment when you want to be heard and understood and the other person wants to be heard or in control? You can't hear ANYTHING they are saying because you are focused on expressing yourself. You miss the fact that you both mean the same thing, only express it differently. That is a pseudo-conflict.

The third type of conflict is content conflict. These are simple conflicts about issues, goals, perceptions, etc. These conflicts can be resolved by getting more information, clarity, new knowledge or compromise. Particularly between partners or teams who need to make decisions on policies, resolve issues, or create new strategies for implementation.

Value conflicts are conflicts over core beliefs, and values that people have held true for a long time. Since core values don't readily change, these disagreements are challenging. The conflict that we have in our current Presidential Administration is about values. They are complex issues like immigration, money, raising children, discipline, religion, government, roles in the family or education. This is where the rubber meets the road, if you will. Often you will see a lot of high emotional expressions with value conflicts because they are personal, and people don't move from their core values, beliefs or philosophies without work.

What is important for us to remember is that conflict is inevitable. Because we are all unique, we will disagree and conflict. The late Overseer Dr. Anderson Culbreath used to say, regarding acknowledging long time wedding anniversaries, that "one of the hardest things to do was keep people together for 25 minutes, no less for 25 years!" Relationships and conflicts are sticky, tricky and risky.

How We Fight

When we approach conflict, the most common result is that there is a winner and a loser. Unless, of course, you are Manny

Pacquiao (Pac Man) or Floyd Mayweather, who must fight to win because it is their job. However, that is not how it always works out. Sometimes both sides lose and other times when both win. Regardless of the type of conflict, we each have a method of handling conflict that is often learned from our first families. It is also part of our nature. We can learn to be responsive or reactive. We can learn to agree to disagree or to be argumentative. We can learn to be passive or assertive. We can learn these behaviors. Understanding this should offer reassurance that if your way of responding to conflict is not healthy for you and those that you encounter, it can be unlearned.

There are five different styles of handling conflict, according to researchers. Competing, avoiding, accommodation, compromise, and collaboration. Competing is the type of conflict that results in one loser and one winner. Avoiding is when one denies that there is an issue, hides their true feelings or tries to play it down.

Accommodating is done by those who want to appease others. They downplay the conflict to smooth over the issues and make it appear easy. Being the person who always submits to the other in the argument just for the sake of making them happy is unhealthy and quite destructive. Your voice is valuable. Your position is valuable. You deserve to be heard.

It's important for the health of your self-esteem, that we speak up for ourselves in relationships and not compromise or accommodate so that others are satisfied. Compromise is negotiating on both sides of the issue to reach a resolution.

While each of these styles is necessary and effective at times, the most beneficial is collaboration. Collaboration is a solution-focused style of handling conflict. Individuals on both sides of the conflict work together to find the best solution for everyone. It is a win-win situation. In interpersonal relationships, everyone can win. It takes effort and can be challenging, but when possible, pursue a collaboration. In a win-win or win-with situation, each side compromises something and benefits in the end. It is helpful to refer to the areas you agree upon first, to create an open dialogue from a positive position. Then begin addressing the areas of dispute. The energy in the conflict is different and the outcome when you begin by focusing on what you agree on or why you said "yes" in the beginning. It helps you to seek a resolution from a place of strength and togetherness rather than weakness and discord.

Have you ever met someone who likes to argue for the sake of argument? They never get to the point of resolution. It's not really their goal. The goal is more of conversation, fighting, making an argument, talking down to you, making you feel embarrassed, taking the floor, etc. It's always about just being in an argument. If you know your partner likes to argue for the sake of arguing with no real effort to resolve anything, you don't have to submit to the argument. Choose not to engage in that unhealthy behavior. It's fruitless. If you know that your friend or partner learned how to argue from their highly combative mother or argumentative father, then you have an advantage. Choose your battles. When they go low, you go high! Just as you learned how to engage in conflict, you can also unlearn those behaviors and employ more healthy solutions.

GIRL, GET YO' LIFE!

12 CONCLUSION

It is one of the beautiful compensations of life that no man can sincerely try to help another without helping himself.
-Ralph Waldo Emerson

This book is by no means an all-inclusive resource. It is, however, a tool to help as you journey through life. The world needs each of our gifts and the abundance that we have to offer it. Trust me when I tell you that the journey is worth the time and energy you give to it. Do your work. Peel back the layers of your onion and get to the core. Life begins there. Study yourself and become a master of you. Discover your life's assignment. Then, use those to cultivate and enrich your own life and the lives of those you love and serve daily.

As we endeavor to live this life with grace, I believe that ultimately, we all want to be healthy and live a life that is meaningful and fulfilling and with people whom we love and serve. In order to pursue and maintain those, we must not overlook that fact that our identity, affects our purpose which has a direct impact on EVERY relationship that we have. None is exempt. Making the effort to get on the journey to self-awareness and discover what you are designed to offer the world is your responsibility. We need your instrument in the orchestra to make the harmony of our world.

AFFIRM YOURSELF DAILY

If you want to begin to see yourself differently and begin to shift the direction of your life, one very powerful practice that you can implement immediately is daily affirmations. I encourage you to incorporate positive, affirming declarations into your daily routine- morning, midday or evening. Remember that your voice is the one your mind hears most often. Speak life to yourself and realign your course. Below is a list of a few to help you begin or to jar your creativity. You may speak them verbatim, or you can add details such as:

I am a woman... of grace and purpose.
I am beautiful... on the inside where God's love resonates from me.

I am creative.
I am magnetic.
I am smart.
I am capable.
I seek to learn more about myself daily.
I am wise.
I am an achiever.
I am chosen.
I am debt free.
I am valuable.
I am whole.
I am forgiving.
I am complete.
I am purposed.

I am unique.
I have people skills.
I am responsible.
I am a rarity.
I am strong.
I am balanced.
I have a sound mind.
I have a voice.
My voice is important.
Others benefit from me.
I make good choices for myself.
I am a master of me.
I am resourceful.
I am a problem solver.
I am conscientious.
I am an incubator.
I am influential.
I am nurturing.
I choose to live freely.
I am healthy.
I am a student of life.
I am a servant.
I am a leader.
I am empowered.
I am powerful.
I am honest.
I am agreeable.
I am reliable.
I am dependable.
I am wealthy.
I am a solution to someone's need.
I am an answer to someone's prayer.

I am a prize.
I am treasured.
I am beautiful.
I am confident.
I am free.
I am supportive.
I am compassionate.
I am optimistic.
I am peaceful.
I am peaceable.
I am perfectly imperfect.
I learn every day.
I am forgiven.
I am loved.
I am an overcomer.
I am courageous.
I am unstoppable.
I am a Masterpiece.

ENDNOTES

1. Hocker, J. L., & Wilmot, W. W. (1995). Interpersonal conflict (p. 21). Madison, WI: Brown & Benchmark.

2. Hergovich, A., Sirch, U., & Felinger, M. (2002). Self-appraisals, actual appraisals and reflected appraisals or pre-adolescent children. Social Behavior and Personality, 30, 603-612

3. Kenny, D. A. (1988). Interpersonal Perception: A Social Relations Analysis. Journal of Social and Personal Relationships, 5(2), 247–261. https://doi.org/10.1177/026540758800500207

4. Bachman, G. F., & Guerrero, L. K. (2006). Relational quality and communicative responses following hurtful events in dating relationships: An expectancy violations analysis. Journal of Social and Personal Relationships, 23(6), 943–963. https://doi.org/10.1177/0265407506070476

5. Munroe, M. (1992). In pursuit of purpose. Destiny Image Publishers.

6. Chapman, G. (2009). The five love languages: How to express heartfelt commitment to your mate. Moody Publishers.

7. Bible, H. (1996). The Holy Bible: King James Version. Broadman & Holman Publishers.

8. Redrick, Mia, The Mom Strategist, Master Business and Life Coach

9. HISTORY. (2019). *World Trade Center*. [online] https://www.history.com/topics/landmarks/world-trade-center [Accessed 24 Apr. 2019].

10. Abuse Defined. (2019). Abuse Defined | The National Domestic Violence Hotline. [online] The National Domestic Violence Hotline. Available at: https://www.thehotline.org/is-this-abuse/abuse-defined/ [Accessed 24 Apr. 2019].

11. Covey, S. (2015). First Things First. Mango Media.

12. Miller, D. P., Waldfogel, J., & Han, W. J. (2012). Family meals and child academic and behavioral outcomes. Child development,83(6),2104–2120. https://doi.org/10.1111/j.1467-8624.2012.01825.x

ABOUT THE AUTHOR

Energetic. Passionate. Intelligent. Witty. Insightful. Relatable. Rachelle encompasses all these characteristics. As a graduate of the University of Cincinnati, she holds a master's degree in Communication. She is particularly passionate about interpersonal communication and the family. In 2012, Rachelle founded At The Table Communication, LLC., whose mission is to support the preservation of the family through education, personal and leadership development of young women ages 16-25. Believing that educating women and girls is the way to change a family, community, nation and world. At The Table Communication (ATTC) provides personal development, relationship education and empowerment workshops and more. To lie in the gap for the diminishing family values, ATTC offers holistic programming to develop the whole person.

Dear Beautiful Young Woman,

I see you! I understand you. How, you ask? Because I once was you. Now, I am here to serve you.

You are always remembered, treasured and forever in my heart and prayers,

Rachelle

GIRL, GET YO' LIFE!

This song speaks to the mission of ATTC, at its core. Read. Listen to it and enjoy.

Can Anybody See Her by Casting Crowns (Lyrics)

She is running
A hundred miles an hour
In the wrong direction
She is trying
But the canyons ever widening
In the depths of her cold heart
So she sets out on another misadventure just to find
She's another two years older and she's three more steps behind

Chorus
Does anybody hear her?
Can anybody see?
Or does anybody even know she's going down today?
Under the shadow of our steeple
With all the lost and lonely people
Searching for the hope that's tucked away in you and me
Does anybody hear her?
Can anybody see?

She is yearning
For shelter and affection
That she never found at home
She is searching
For a hero to ride in,
To ride in and save the day
And then walks in her prince charming
And he knows just what to say

GIRL, GET YO' LIFE!

A momentary lapse of reason
And she gives herself away

Chorus
Does anybody hear her?
Can anybody see?
Or does anybody even know she's going down today?
Under the shadow of our steeple
With all the lost and lonely people
Searching for the hope that's tucked away in you and me
Does anybody hear her?
Can anybody see?

If judgment looms under every steeple
If lofty glances from lofty people
Who can't see past her scarlet letter
And we never even met her
If judgment looms under every steeple
If lofty glances from lofty people
Who can't see past her scarlet letter
And we never even met her
Never even met her

Chorus 2x
He is running a hundred miles an hour in the wrong direction

Songwriters: Mark Hall
© Sony/ATV Music Publishing LLC, ESSENTIAL MUSIC PUBLISHING, CAPITOL CHRISTIAN MUSIC GROUP

Additional Resources

The Holy Bible – King James Version or Amplified Version

The Five Love Languages: Dr Gary Chapman

The Assignment: Dr. Mike Murdock

The Four Agreements: Miguel Ruiz

Single, Separated, Married, and Life After Divorce: Dr. Myles Munroe

Avoiding Mr. Wrong and What to Do if You Didn't: Dr. Steven Arterburn

Boundaries: Dr. Henry Cloud and Dr. John Townsend

Do What You Are – Discover the Perfect Career for You Through the Secrets of Personality Types: Paul Tieger

What Color is Your Parachute: Richard N. Bolles

What to Say When You Talk to Yourself: Dr. Shad Helmstetter

Now, Discover Your Strengths: Marcus Buckingham and Donald O. Clifton

Think and Grow Rich: Napoleon Hill

Introvert Power: Laurie Helgoe

Connect with Me!

- Visit my website at www.rachellelawson.com
- Download, listen and share my FREE podcast: **Rachelle's Corner** on Spotify, Apple Podcasts, Google Podcasts, Anchor & PocketCasts
- Join my FREE Facebook community by signing up at bit.ly/connectwithrachelle
- For more information and to enroll in the course: *Just Be Yourself!* Visit bit.ly/justbeyourself
- Join the Intentional Living Membership group at bit.ly/connectwithrachelle
- **Book me to speak** at your next women's event, graduation, or conference by emailing atthetablecommunication@gmail.com

More from the Author Coming Soon

Girl Get Yo' Life! Life Activity Workbook (Spring 2019)

Girl, Get Yo' Life! A Young Woman's Guide to Life and Relationships that Win (Volume Two) (TBD)

A Conduit for His Grace: A Memoir (for mothers of fatherless children) (Fall 2019)

101 Reasons You Are Worth It (TBD)

GIRL, GET YO' LIFE!

www.ingramcontent.com/pod-product-compliance
Lightning Source LLC
Chambersburg PA
CBHW021411290426
44108CB00010B/482